Muses

Sophie Valentic

BookLeaf Publishing

Presentation by *BookLeaf Publishing*

Web: www.bookleafpub.com

E-mail: info@bookleafpub.com

ISBN: 9789357212045

First edition 2023

DEDICATION

Muses is dedicated to the muses of history. The storytellers, both the forgotten and the famous, and their subjects. May their stories live on.

ACKNOWLEDGEMENT

Thanks to my family, for helping my through this. Special thanks to my mother, who helped me edit these late at night. Love you mum. Thanks also to my inspirations, I'm not sure I couldn't done it without you.

Little Bird

Little bird, singing in the tree.
Do you regret being free?
Little bird, flying high.
Regret the day you were born to die.
Funny little bird, you sing so sweet.
Rue the day you made me weep.
Poor little bird, with its broken wing.
Do you finally feel life's sting?
Dead little bird, lying on the ground.
Do you regret being found?

Purpose

Am I here to be used?
Abused to amuse the enthused crowd?
Am I here to be cherished?
Fetishised as I perish at their wish?
Or am I here for my passion
That I ration into rationed compassion?
Could it be that I'm here to learn,
To turn this burning concern into something I
can use?
Am I here to flourish,
To nourish the ravished world until it's
replenished?
Am I here to be an authority?
To give priority to those with superiority?

I cannot give the answer, for I do not know,
Why we undergo the plateau of life.
I cannot comprehend the trend of existence,
To defend, pretend, or be a friend,
But then again, no one can.
But in the end,
Whether I ascend or descend,
The answer I can recommend is 42.

Moments of Love

Infinite, boundless,
Forever by my side.
Both there being my guide.
A Northern star,
The guiding light,
A voice of care,
Through all my life.

A quiet night,
Only crickets and the
buzz of electricity between us.
Solemn conversations,
To laughter and joy.
Whispered secrets,
Classified knowledge,
Rants about history, myths and truth,
I think, all I need is you.
Sunday morning,
Eggs and bacon,
Singing to guitar,
Yours and mine,
Playing anything and everything.
"Watch Over Me" is sung twice,
A memory of home,
Half forgotten.

I think, all I need is this.

My mother and my father,
My guides in life.
My guardian, my protector,
My mother and father.
Quiet moments and raucous laughter,
Are all moments of love.

The Kitchen

I whirl around the kitchen,
Plait whipping around me.
One thing after another,
Never stopping.
Hands grasping for vegetables,
Carrot and celery and broccoli.
Fill a bowl with meat,
Toss the chicken tub into the sink,
Replace it.
Keep going.
Find a spot to put the uncooked food.
Lid the containers,
Bag up the orders,
Move on to the next thing.
Order the fried food,
Hand grasp for vegetables,
Fill a bowl with lamb.
Find a spot.
Keep going.
Move.
Move.
Move.
Lunge to grab a sauce.
Send the order out.
Check the time.

5 minutes late.
Move,
Move.
Move.
I am a whirlwind,
Calling orders,
Preparing food,
Bagging orders.
I keep everything in check as I work.
I never stop.
Not once.

By the end of the night, I am sore.
My feet hurt, and I'm covered in sweat.
My plait is messy, my clothes a mess.
I rest.
Tomorrow I will do it all again.

Remember Me

Does anything even matter when all you know is
pain?
Does anything even matter when nobody knows
your name?
Does anything even matter when everything
stays the same?
Does it even matter when everything changes?

All I know is that someone will know my name,
That they will remember me when the world
ends in flame.
Good or bad, known as brilliant or a shame,
I swear that one day, you will know my name.

I will set the world aflame,
I will take all the blame,
I don't care what I do,
But someone will remember my name.

I refuse to be lost in the sands of time,
I refuse to be forgotten,
My name erased,
My achievements gone.
I will carve them in stone,
I will write them in bone.

I will ensure I am known.

I will make sure I matter, even if all I know is pain.
I will make sure I matter and everyone knows my name.
I will make sure I matter if everything stays the same.
I know I will matter if I make everything change.

Us

I have never met a calm teenager.
We have rage written in our bones
And pain burnt into our hearts.
Yet you do not listen.
We have seen our friends die,
Children taught to run at shooters,
To give others just a few more seconds.

No one mentions that more people died
In Hurricane Maria than 9/11.
You can't use hurricanes to justify war.
But we are here.
We see, and we will change it.

We grew up with stories of pain,
How we will never own a home.
We will rise from the ashes,
Create a world of hope,
Because the world burnt around us.
We will do it because we have nothing to lose.

We were born with information at our fingertips.
Yet you told us to be quiet.
You said the adults were talking.
But we are adults now.

Now we get to talk,
Our lungs will be shredded,
Voices shattered with the words we speak.
You had your chance.
Now it’s our turn.

What It Looks Like

It’s not supposed to look like this
That’s what they say
That’s not what it looks like on TV
You dont look like the movie stars
So clearly, your ok
Why wouldn’t you be in the first place

Your room is a mess,
You don't have tear stains,
Your hair isn’t clean,
Your not endlessly crying
You’re fine.

But I am apathetic,
My hobbies aren’t mine anymore.
I am lost and scared,
I don’t care if I die anymore.

But still, they say
This isn’t what it looks like.
Where are your tears of eternal sadness?
Where is your makeup,
Artfully smudged?
You must be fine.
You have no reason not to be.

Hope in the Dark

It's so surreal,
Sitting in the dark.
Nothing left,
But hope

Hope for a brighter future,
Hope for better days,
Hope for all that missing,
Hope for all that's grey.

In the dark,
We sit.
We hide and hope,
And pray and dream,
In the dark.

Cause I hope,
For better days,
For better night,
For all that I've lost,
In the dark

Realisations

I realised I loved you in a moment,
Between one thought and the next,
I knew.
You laughed, glancing at me,
And I knew.
We sang together,
Melodies and voices intertwine,
Like they should never be apart.
And I knew.
The whispers we shared,
Quiet moments between us,
The murmur of "spiked" at a party.
Muttering our grievances,
We shared our dreams, and I knew.

I knew I loved you then.
Between years of laughter,
at our faults and successes,
Frustration over people,
Who just wouldn't leave.
Moments of shared joy and sorrow,
Our dreams, our secrets, our regrets.
Through it all,
I loved you.

And as you laugh again, looking at me,
Bright and full or broken and hollow,
I know that I love you.

How Can I Be Loved

I know that you love me,
Believe me, I do,
But I get this feeling,
A hurt in my chest,
A tug in my gut,
That you're lying.

How can I be loved?
How can I,
The gold in the night,
The purple and yellow,
The bland, the basic,
Be loved?
Me, the lover of true crime,
The dramatic historian,
The hater of movies.
How can I be loved?
I am not interesting,
My blood is not mixed,
Not overly pretty or extremely lucky.
My family is basic,
What you'd expect.
There's no tragedy,
No story,
Nothing to make me interesting.

You ask, “How can you be loved?”
You, who has
The sea crashing against rocks in your eyes,
The stars shimmering in your smile,
The universe smiles when you laugh,
And cries when you’re sad,
And you ask how can you be loved?
You, who can talk about anything,
Who gets invested in everything,
Who laughs so easily, talks so smoothly.
You, who charms everyone you meet.
And you ask how you can be loved.

She

She is my hopes and dreams.
The air beneath my wings,
Letting me fly to her.
Cause she is my light and life,
My only fire
Keeping me safe from the dark.

Things I Wish I Said

Things I wish I said.
"You make me feel alive."
Things I wish I did.
Kissed you that night.
Things I wish you said.
"I love you."
Things I wish you did.
Stayed.

But here's what happened.
We danced chest to chest, spinning,
You dipped me, black on lilac.
We laughed as you pulled me back up.
I wish I had kissed you then.
I wish I went with you when you left.
We met up the next day and the week after that.

I knew it couldn't last forever, but I ached.
I ached for your touch, your smiles, your laughter.
I ache for you.
You said you wanted me too.
And you promised you wouldn't fuck me over.

Here's how it ended.

We danced again, in a cheap pub.
Spun again, green on yellow.
I dropped down low as you swung your hips.
Someone showed you what a cheerleader does,
You were dressed as one.
They laughed at us,
As we kissed.
This time I went with you.
Sometimes I wish I didn't.
Others, I'm just glad I got to spend a night with you.
We watched horror movies,
I hated them before,
I didn't then,
I do now.

The next day, as I was leaving you pulled me away
"It isn't fair to you,
It isn't fair to me."
I know.
I knew it had to end someday.
I know I was a spring fling.
I don't care.
I didn't care then, and I don't care now.
I want you.
I still do.

So the things I wish I said.

“I don’t care.”
Things I wish I did.
Kissed you goodbye.
Things I wish I said.
“We can make it work.”
Things I wish you did.
Agreed.

Cold Water

Cold water is like ice.
Ice chilling the bones,
Burning the skin.
Cold water is limbs going numb,
Fingers going red,
Tingling with frostnip,
Frostbite setting in,
A blizzard entering your lungs,
Whenever you try to take a breath.
It burns like fire when you don't.
Even if you escape,
Cold water is hell.

You freeze from the outside in.
Your ears and nose go first,
Then your fingers and toes.
It spreads up your limbs,
Your body diverting warmth to its core,
Attempting to keep you alive.
Your body dies slowly.
Your skin is warmer
As it slowly turns white with cold.
Your body numbs,
Cold, pain and discomfort mean nothing.
Your joints stop,

You can no longer move.

You stop shivering,
Shudders giving way to stillness,
Your body saving energy.
You dose off constantly,
Your breathing slows,
You get confused.
Who are you?
Where are you?
Why are you so cold?
Your reflexes slow,
Your coordination,
Not as fine as before.
You begin to feel warmer,
After a while.
You're hot, overheating in all these layers.
You begin to take off your clothes,
Clumsy movements baring more skin to the cold.
You freeze further.

When they find you,
They find you naked,
Ice frozen to your skin,
Limbs almost fully white.
As your body warms,
Your limbs go black and hard,
Frozen and dead.

They puff up, forming blisters.
Your limbs have decayed away.
Even if you leave it,
Cold water is hell.

Humanity

What is it to have a conscious?
Is it the ability to feel?
To have empathy?
But what about whales?
Humpbacks who save seals,
Carrying them on their bellies,
Safe from the orcas below.
Is it to feel grief?
But elephants mourn their dead,
Return to sites years after,
Even for humans.
Is it to think?
To use logic?
But crows use water displacement.
The ability to prepare for possibilities?
Octopi use coconut shells as portable armour,
Carrying it until needed.
Tool use?
Otters use rocks to open hard shells.
Drug use?
Dolphins use pufferfish to get high.
What defines having a consciousness?
Is it morals?
Some wolves will kill others,
Some will let them live after beating them.

Orcas will torture seals,
Flinging them in the air with their tails.
These animals have consciousness.
So what about humanity?

Apollo

"The sun inside of him could set the kingdom ablaze; he knows this, he does. And he still asks me to love him, to face the flame. Find me in the ashes."
— Emily Palermo

He is golden,
Light personified.
A deity that the world,
Cannot help but love.

I cannot stop my love for him.
I want to go everywhere with him.
I know it will burn.
I know my skin will shrivel up,
And blacken as he gets too close.
I cannot bring myself to care.
I still love him.

They are love,
Mortality personified,
Not afraid to live,
Uncaring if they die.

I cannot help my love for them.

I want to take them everywhere.
I can see them burn.
Eyes glowing gold,
My power burning through their soul.
I must leave them.
For I cannot let them die.

So we watch each other from afar.
He burns twice as bright,
Ebony skin radiant in the light
Their eyes shimmer gold,
Bright amber glowing with my light.
We can never touch.
So we content ourselves with seeing.
Watching from afar.
As they eventually age and die,
And Apollo stays the same,
He will never gift another with glowing eyes.

Menin

"Sing, goddess, of the wrath of Achilles, son of Peleus."

I will sing of wrath.
A river of rage,
Burning everything in its path.
A tornado of flame,
Flickers lashing out at everyone around.
A red haze over ones vision,
Blurring the world,
Shrinking empathy to a pinprick.
Yet no one cares.
The hatred overwhelms all.
Everything is consumed,
Leaving only the ashes of the past behind.
The ashes and coals cool, blown away by the wind,
Leaving only the empty numbness of what could be shame.

I will sing of wrath,
A blizzard of biting fury,
Nipping at the heels.
Cold glares and frosty silences.
Ignoring the people around us.

A cold fury, the eye in the storm.
A grudge held for months, years.
A memory never truly forgotten.
Things brought up in fights years later.
A cruel smile, a chilling laugh.
Watching as everyone falls around them.
Everything is frozen.
The world around them cracks and shatters.
All that remains is the memories of what
might've been warmth.

I will sing of wrath.
Mine and others.
Fury that bites and burns equally.
My rage does not burn loud.
My wrath does not scream of hatred.
My fury burns cold.
Yet my hatred burns like the sun,
Shrivelling everything in its path.
My wrath cannot be tamed.
My wrath can only be directed.
I will direct it.
I will sing of my wrath
as I fill the river with bodies.
Bodies of the cruel, the heartless,
The rapists, the murderers.
The river will be filled with them.
For I will sing of my wrath.

Icarus

"Never regret thy fall,
O Icarus of the fearless flight,
For the greatest tragedy of them all,
Is never to feel the burning light." -Oscar Wilde

I am Icarus,
Lover of the sun,
Though I ever only loved him once,
And cannot be the only one.

Icarus fell,
He loved too hard,
I am stuck in this cell,
Left guarded and scarred.

I do not care,
For if I never tried,
I would be in despair,
Having died inside.

I saw the world,
From the poor man's perspective,
And so I unfurled,
My planned directive.

For how could I fly,
If I never had jumped?
How could I know,
If I never even tried?

And so I will try,
Against all odds,
And I will achieve my goals,
No matter the cost.

Sinners

I hunger,
My stomach aches,
Never fully full.
I eat and drink,
Yet it is never enough.
I grow larger and larger,
Until I cannot walk.
I continue to eat,
I continue to talk.
I talk about phobia,
How planes aren't inclusive,
How I'm bullied online,
Saying my eating is abusive.
I cannot stop,
I eat, and I eat.
I end up on TV,
I had a heart attack at 23.

I sleep, and I sleep,
Through day and night.
I can never stop sleeping,
Or lying about.
I watch Netflix and Stan,
Hulu and Disney,
Anything to stay,

Off my feet.
I do not shower,
I do not eat.
Everything is tiring,
So all I do is sleep.
One day I am buried,
Simply by mistake,
I sleep through the funeral,
The burial, the wake.
I wake up in that coffin and cannot escape.

I whisper and wait,
In the wings for you,
Glowing eyes,
Of emerald green hue.
I stare at your laugh,
Your smile, your face,
I want to spread your guts
All over the place.
So one day, I buy,
A Glock just for you.
I practice and prepare,
All ready for you.
I invite you over,
With a snake-like tongue,
And finally when I,
Am ready to fire,
You hit me upside the back of the head.

I sneer at the people,
My workers below,
Slaving away
for my platinum throne.
They are the weak,
Made to be oppressed.
They are the poor,
They work without rest.
I am a god.
The best of the best.
I stay in my tower,
Watching the world below.
The weak, the pitiful,
They do not know,
I'm the only individual.
I stand above them all,
I scream as I fall.

Jewellery litters my skin,
Diamonds cover my heart,
As I buy more priceless art.
Another I must add to my hoard.
Another I must add to the score.
The score of tallies,
Gifts given, not received.
Gold drips off my skin,
Not a place is left bare,
Eventually though,
I start to tire.

The cuffs around my wrists,
Begin to grow tighter,
The chains around my neck,
Begin to go taut.
I claw at my throat, scratching and scraping,
My gold has betrayed me, as I choke on an earring.

I do not stop.
The hunger grows,
Shivering up my spine.
It loosens,
a white light behind my eyes.
I continue.
The men keep coming, never halting.
I beg for more. I need more.
Heat curls in my stomach again,
In my womb.
They continue.
I fall asleep to new men using my body.
Using me.
I wake up, one of the men choking me.
I push for more, harder, the heat drowning me.
They keep pushing past my limits,
until I pass out in their arms a final time.

I hate them.
I hate them all.
I will kill them.

Getting a gun is easy.
Getting it into the club is easier.
I fire into the crowd,
Bullets flying,
blood spraying across my face,
Screams reaching my ears.
I cackle.
Finally, they realise.
Bodies litter the floor,
Men and women alike,
Possessed by what they call 'love.'
I turn away from the crowd.
I do not regret anything.
I grin as I shoot, and laugh as I am shot.

We are the sins.
The sins of life.
The sins of humanity.
We are the gluttonous,
Those who eat themselves to death,
Under the guise of 'body positivity.'
We are the slothful,
Those who have no work ethic,
Who sleep their lives away.
We are the envious,
Those who crave what we don't have,
Never realising what we do.
We are the arrogant,
Who stand above the rest,

Not understanding that they aren't worth less.
We are the greedy,
Those who gild themselves in gold,
Not recognising their own value.
We are the lustful,
The lonely and empty,
We fill the gaps with pleasure and pain.
We are the wrathful,
The raging fire that burns through our lives,
Ashes are all that remain.
We are the sins.
The sins of life.
The sins of humanity.
We are your sins.

The Gods Are Dead

The Gods are dead.
Zeus lurks in seedy bars,
Eyes lingering on too-young waitresses,
Offering spiked drinks to girls who flinch away,
And boys who don't.

Hera waits in the wings,
Glaring at the people Zeus brings back,
Watching over her children,
While damning those who aren't.

Poseidon walks the seashore over and over again,
Picking up the same pieces of plastic as before,
His domain shining rainbow in the sunrise,
Slick with another oil spill.

Demeter walks the fields and streets,
Crying about GMOs and medication,
Preaching essential oils and diffusers,
While her daughter dies of Polio next door.

Ares roams the streets of demolished villages,
Bodies litter the ground, women and children,
A senseless slaughter of their own people.

There is no glory in war.

Athena writes scathing political pieces.
She writes about strategy and power,
The ones she wants to convince don't believe
her.
She wishes they would remove their blindfolds.

Aphrodite scrolls through Tinder,
Creates another profile, always swiping right.
She knows they only want her for sex.
She can't bring herself to care.

Hephstaphus stumbles out of his workshop.
People love his work, pay hundreds for
delicate gears crafted by giant hands.
They still sneer at his limp.

Apollo sings constantly,
His performances entrance the crowd,
They flock to him like the sun,
He mourns his lost loves in his songs.

Artemis gets into fights daily.
She and her girls stalk the night,
hunting men like her father, protecting the
innocent.
She wishes she didn't have to.

Hermes delivers another package to another house.
They won't realise it's empty until after he's moved on.
On to another town, always moving, never slowing.
He used to find joy in this.

Dionysis flips between serving drinks and crazy rants,
Laughing with customers and sobbing in the corner.
Some say listening to his ramblings causes insanity,
He wishes it didn't.

Persephone dances in Autumn and Spring,
Her summer is spent with her obsessive mother,
her winters with her loving husband.
She doesn't think about Minthe.

Hades wanders graveyards and museums,
Lecturing anyone who'll listen about the dead.
People still die, but he no longer rules them.
He finally gets to spend time with his wife.

Hestia watches them.
Her hearth is always open to her family,
Even if no one believes in it.

She hopes they'll return.

The old gods are dead.
We are all that remains.

www.ingramcontent.com/pod-product-compliance
Lightning Source LLC
Chambersburg PA
CBHW062109140826
49812CB00058B/965
9789357212045